WITHDRAWN

MILITARY ENGINEERING IN ACTION

MILITARY RIFLES
COMBAT READY

Taylor Baldwin Kiland and Gerry Souter

Enslow Publishing
101 W. 23rd Street
Suite 240
New York, NY 10011
USA

enslow.com

Published in 2016 by Enslow Publishing, LLC.
101 W. 23rd Street, Suite 240, New York, NY 10011

Copyright © 2016 by Enslow Publishing, LLC.

All rights reserved.

No part of this book may be reproduced by any means without the written permission of the publisher.

Library of Congress Cataloging-in-Publication Data

Kiland, Taylor Baldwin, 1966–
 Military rifles : combat ready / Taylor Baldwin Kiland and Gerry Souter.
    pages cm. —(Military engineering in action)
 Includes bibliographical references and index.
 Summary: "Describes the development, use, and abilities of Humvees in the military"-- Provided by publisher.
 Audience: Grades 7-8.
 ISBN 978-0-7660-6916-9 (library binding)
 ISBN 978-0-7660-7067-7 (pbk.)
 ISBN 978-0-7660-7068-4 (6-pack)
 1. Rifles—United States—Juvenile literature. I. Souter, Gerry. II. Title.
 UD390.K55 2015
 355.8'2425—dc23
                          2015011221

Printed in the United States of America

To Our Readers: We have done our best to make sure all Web site addresses in this book were active and appropriate when we went to press. However, the author and the publisher have no control over and assume no liability for the material available on those Web sites or on any Web sites they may link to. Any comments or suggestions can be sent by e-mail to customerservice@enslow.com.

Portions of this book originally appeared in *Military Rifles: Fierce Firepower*.

Photo Credits: blackwaterimages/E+/Getty Images, p. 22; brian.ch/Flickr.com/3598148339_7a7c14322d_b.jpg/CC BY 2.0, p. 29; Dieter Spears/E+/Getty Images, p. 4; Everett Historical/Shutterstock.com, p. 13; Fort Worth Star-Telegram/Tribune News Service/Getty Images, p. 17; KristfromGermany/Wikimedia Commons/H&K MP7.jpg/Public Domain, p. 6; J.J. Harrison/Wikimedia Commons/Gallinago stenura - Laem Pak Bia.jpg/CC BY 3.0, p. 16; Lance Corporal Roberto Torres, United States Marine Corps/Wikimedia Commons/USMC Sniper M82.JPEG/Public Domain, p. 33; Militarist/Shutterstock.com, pp. 2, 11, 47; Pfc. Han-byeol Kim/defenseimagery.mil/Wikimedia Commons/U.S. Army 2nd Lt. Hannah Drosehn, a quartermaster officer assigned to the 70th Brigade Support Battalion, 210thFires Brigade, 2nd Infantry Division, looks down her sight on the M16A2 rifle as she waits to 130319-A-WG463-056.jpg/Public Domain, p. 42; Schlomo Polonsky/Hemera/Thinkstock, p. 10; Shutterstock.com (art/backgrounds throughout book): Dianka Pyzhova, Ensuper, foxie, kasha_malasha, pashabo; Spc. Henry/Wikimedia Commons/Barret M82 DA-ST 92 07336.jpg/Public Domain, p. 34; Terry Moore/Stocktreck Images/Getty Images, p. 7; US Air Force, p. 20; US Army, pp. 9, 27, 28, 43; US Army photo by Forest Berkshire, US Army Accessions Command, p. 44; US Army photo by Michael Molinaro, USAMU PAO, p. 39; US Army photo by Pfc. Kissta M. Feldner, 2BCT, 82D ABN DIV, PAO SPC, p. 41; US Army photo by Pfc. Micah E. Clare, p. 32; US Army photo by Sgt. Joshua Laidacker, p. 36; US Army photo by Specialist Seth LaCount, p. 24; US Army photo by Staff Sgt. John Zumer, Brigade Combat Team, 1st Infantry Division, p. 9 (right); US Army photo by Staff Sgt. Marshall R. Mason, 5th Signal Command Public Affairs, p. 21; US Marine Corps photo by Cpl. Taylor L. Main, p. 1; US Navy photo by Mass Communications Specialist 3rd Class Ernesto Hernandez Fonte/Wikimedia Commons/US Navy 090815-N-9584H-017 Seabees assigned to the 30th Naval Construction Regiment conduct marksmanship training in Kuwait before deploying to Afghanistan.jpg/Public Domain, p. 38; William Vandivert/The LIFE Picture Collection/Getty Images, p.15.

Cover Credits: US Marine Corps photo by Cpl. Taylor L. Main (front); Shutterstock.com: kasha_malasha (camouflage background), foxie (series logo), Militarist (rifle, back).

CONTENTS

CHAPTER 1   **Rifles: Weapons of Choice**   5

CHAPTER 2   **The History of the Military Rifle** 12

CHAPTER 3   **The M16: The Standard Since 1962** 18

CHAPTER 4   **The M4 and Combat Rifles of the Future** 23

CHAPTER 5   **Saved by a Sniper** 30

CHAPTER 6   **Developing Shooting Skills** 37

Timeline 45

Glossary 46

Further Reading 47

Index 48

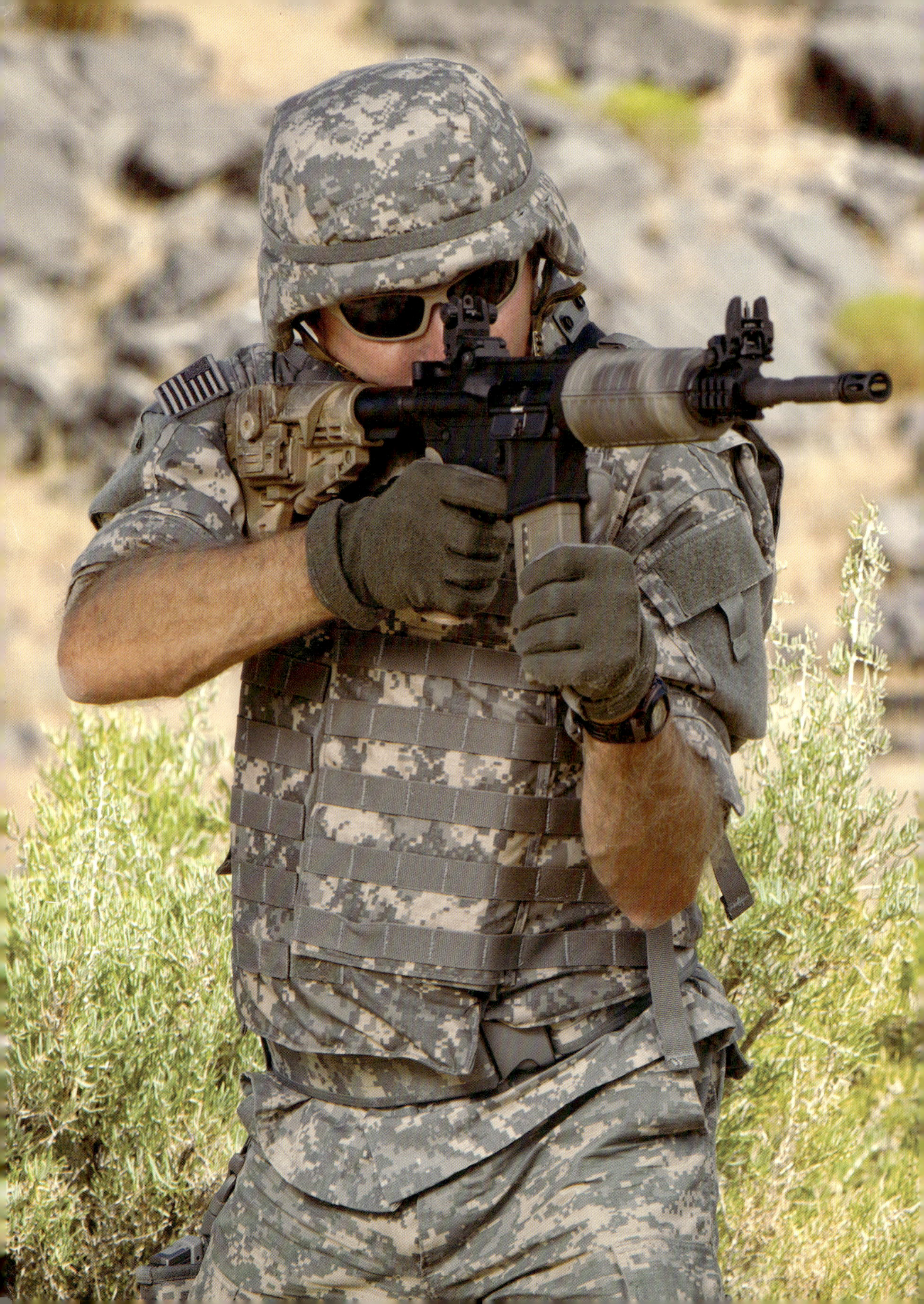

CHAPTER 1

Rifles: Weapons of Choice

It was a warm night with little moonlight in May 2011. Two small teams of Navy SEALs from the Naval Special Warfare Development Group (or DEVGRU) flew over the border from Afghanistan to Pakistan in two CH-47 Chinook helicopters, heading for a residential compound in the town of Abbottabad. The men didn't talk much. They knew their mission, Operation Neptune Spear, was going to require all their concentration, energy, training, and expertise. They also knew that the mission was extremely dangerous and they might die in the attempt. They were on their way to a raid on Osama bin Laden's hideout.

The mastermind behind the September 11, 2001, attacks on the World Trade Center and the Pentagon, bin Laden had been on the hit list of the United States ever since. Now, the military and the Central Intelligence Agency (CIA) were confident they had found him. The SEALs were tasked with killing this most notorious and dangerous

MILITARY RIFLES: Combat Ready

terrorist. Their primary weapons for the mission? Rifles—most likely Heckler & Koch MP7 military assault rifles.

Hovering over the destination, the first helicopter crashed inside the compound and the second helicopter safely landed outside the compound. Uninjured and wearing night vision goggles, the SEALs quickly regrouped and entered the house, not knowing how many people they would encounter or how heavily armed they would be. The CIA had cut the power to the neighborhood, so none of the residents could turn on the lights and they probably could not see their assailants. The SEALs searched room by room and finally found bin Laden on the third floor hiding behind his wife, where they instantly killed him with rifles customized for just such a mission. They took his body with them and jumped back into their helicopters and flew back to Afghanistan. The entire mission took thirty-eight minutes.

The Modern Combat Rifle

The US military counts on the firepower and strength of the modern combat rifle. One of the newest rifles, the M4, was introduced to the US Marines in 2002. It has become the standard weapon of the US Army and Marine Corps. It is a shorter, lighter, and more

This MP7A1 has a laser aiming module.

A US Marine wears a night vision device to allow him to see in the dark.

MILITARY RIFLES: Combat Ready

practical version of the M16, a military rifle used around the world. The M16 was a huge step forward in military rifle design when it was introduced in the United States in the 1960s. It is the perfect example of how rifles have been improved over the years to keep up with new technology. The M4 is the latest in a long line of military rifles that have constantly been improved to help make US soldiers the best in the world.

Winning battles has often required soldiers on foot to occupy the opposing force's land. These soldiers need weapons that can defeat that opposing force in both close fighting and from some distance away. For a military rifle like the M4 to do these jobs, it must have several features:

1. It must be rugged and able to withstand mud, sand, water, explosions, extreme cold and extreme heat, and being dropped.

2. It must be reliable and able to shoot on a target over long and short distances, called ranges, of 82 to 984 feet (25 to 300 meters), whenever a soldier picks it up.

3. It must shoot powerfully over long distances and must be able to fire a bullet that will stop opposing soldiers. The bullet must shatter against hard surfaces so it does not bounce and injure innocent civilians (nonmilitary people).

4. The military rifle must be light enough to carry and easy to use for many different jobs. These include fighting over long distances in the desert, up close in rooms and hallways in buildings, in cities, and where trails are narrow between thick bushes and trees.

Every American soldier must accept the tremendous responsibility that goes with carrying a deadly weapon. From the American Revolution to the present, American soldiers have fought to protect people's rights and liberties. Many soldiers have given their lives in battle so others could be free. The one weapon every soldier must master to win these battles is the military rifle.

FACT

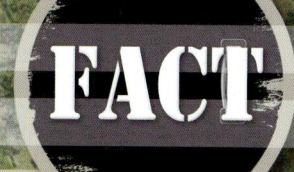

Rifles vs. Guns

In the military, the word "gun" is not used to refer to a rifle. A "rifle" is a firearm with a rifled, or grooved, barrel, such as the M4. The word "gun" refers to a cannon-type weapon. The large M119 Howitzer is a gun that is commonly used by the army today.

An M4 rifle (top) and an M119 Howitzer (right)

FACT

Millimeters, Inches, and Calibers

Military ammunition is always named after its diameter in millimeters. For example, a 7.62 millimeter (mm) bullet is 7.62mm in diameter. Outside of the military, the term "caliber" refers to a similar measurement, but in inches. A 7.62mm bullet is about .30 inches in diameter, or .30 caliber. In other words, a 7.62mm military bullet is the same as a .30-caliber civilian bullet.

The inside of the rifle's muzzle is also measured in millimeters. Rifle barrels are made to accept bullets of one size only, based on the width of the muzzle. The 5.56mm M16 rifle, for example, can fire only 5.56mm bullets.

M16 rifle ammunition

FACT

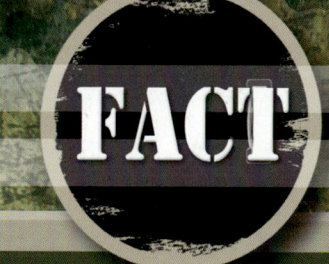

Parts of a Rifle

The modern military rifle has six basic parts:

1. The **stock** supports the rifle against the soldier's shoulder.
2. The **action** is a collection of mechanical parts that make the rifle shoot.
3. The **trigger** connects the finger of the shooter to the mechanism that fires the rifle. Squeezing the trigger with the finger releases the firing pin that fires the ammunition in the rear of the barrel.
4. The **barrel** helps guide the bullets toward the target. The front end of the barrel is called the **muzzle**. The rear of the barrel is called the **breech**.
5. The **sights** help the soldier aim the barrel at the target.
6. The **magazine** holds the rifle's ammunition.

CHAPTER 2

The History of the Military Rifle

Soon after the Chinese invented gunpowder in the ninth century, they invented the first firearm, which was called a fire lance. This weapon combined a spear with a mounted bamboo tube that contained gunpowder and a small projectile or a poison dart. The fire lance had a range of only a few feet. It was the predecessor to all modern firearms.

By the late 1700s, frontiersmen, trappers, and hunters were using hunting rifles made in Kentucky and Pennsylvania. Instead of a smooth tube for a barrel, these weapons had spiral grooves called rifling carved into the inside of their barrels. The grooves dug into the fired bullet as it passed down the barrel. This caused the lead ball, or bullet, to spin as it left the rifle. The spinning made the bullet go straighter and more accurately to a distant target. Rifling was a new invention that had come from Europe.

African-American soldiers aim their rifles at the enemy in Virginia during the Civil War.

MILITARY RIFLES: Combat Ready

In the Revolutionary War (1775–1783), American colonial soldiers used these accurate hunting rifles against their British opponents. They were able to shoot from a distance and stay hidden. British officers fell from their horses not knowing the origin of the Americans' shots. But soon the British were using men called snipers armed with their own accurate rifles against the Americans.

After the Civil War (1861–1865), all combat weapons had rifling in their barrels. Some were loaded from the rear or breech instead of from the muzzle. These "breechloader" rifles used brass or copper cases called cartridges (or rounds). Inside the cartridge was a bullet and the propellant, or gunpowder, that would ignite and explode, forcing the bullet down the barrel and out the end of the rifle. Using cartridges, more shots could be fired faster.

Combat Rifles in the Twentieth Century

Gun designers worked through the following decades to make rifles even more efficient. In 1936 the first semiautomatic military rifle was invented by John Garand. Military rifles before that time fired one shot at a time, and the cartridges, also called rounds, were reloaded by hand. Garand's weapon, called the M1, could fire eight preloaded cartridges, one at a time with each pull of the trigger. American soldiers in World War II (1939–1945) were the only soldiers to have these semiautomatic rifles.

"Semiautomatic" means the rifle can fire multiple shots before reloading, but the trigger has to be pulled once for each shot fired. "Automatic" means that as long as the trigger is held down, the weapon fires until all the ammunition in the magazine is gone.

Later, during the Korean War (1950–1953) and Vietnam War (1959–1975), it became clear that American soldiers would need an automatic weapon—one that was lighter in weight and more rugged. A new military rifle had to be developed.

The US Army wanted its new weapon to have high accuracy for single shots as well as automatic fire. A rifle that had been designed by Eugene Stoner in 1956 fit the bill. It was a stunning change from

The History of the Military Rifle

During World War II, US soldiers were armed with semiautomatic rifles, such as this Garand M1.

standard rifles made of wood and steel. Stoner used aluminum for the casing that housed the operating parts and trigger, called the receiver. Also, the shoulder stock was made of plastic. This resulted in a rifle that weighed only 7 pounds (3.17 kilograms). The M1 weighed more than 9 pounds (4 kg). The rifle also had a built-in carry handle that contained the sights used to aim the shot at a target.

The army had found its new weapon. The M16, as it came to be known, was a very important development in military rifles.

FACT

What Is a Sniper?

The first snipers were men in medieval England who hunted a small, delicate bird called the snipe. The dainty birds were cooked and eaten in meat pies. Specially trained men hid in trees, sometimes under cloaks covered with leaves and twigs. They waited quietly near the birds' nests. These "snipers" then quickly caught the birds with a net.

Riflemen who hid and waited quietly for a target to appear during a battle also eventually became known as snipers, after the bird hunters.

This long-billed bird is a snipe.

FACT

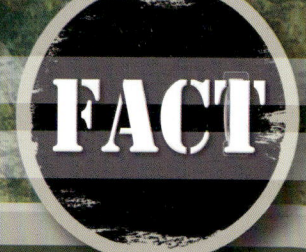

Famous American Snipers

- Hiram Berdan (1824–1893), who commanded the 1st and 2nd US Sharpshooters during the American Civil War.
- Adelbert Waldron (1933–1995), an army sniper with 109 confirmed kills during the Vietnam War.
- Carlos Hathcock (1942–1999), a Marine Corps sniper with 93 confirmed kills during the Vietnam War.
- Chuck Mawhinney (born 1949), a Marine Corps sniper who holds the record for most confirmed kills (103) by a US Marine.
- Chris Kyle (1974–2013), a former Navy SEAL credited with 160 confirmed kills in Iraq, the most career sniper kills in US military history.

Chris Kyle

CHAPTER 3

The M16: The Standard Since 1962

Major Colin Risso of the British army was in trouble, trapped and taking fire from all sides. With bullets raining down and rocket-propelled grenades (RPGs) slamming into his truck, Major Risso jumped into action. He grabbed the nearest rifle, an M16. As he and his fellow soldiers were showered with fire and sharp splinters, he quickly began to return fire.

Major Risso had been traveling with a convoy, or group of vehicles, with both British and American troops in Bagram, Afghanistan. They had just descended down an embankment into a narrow, dry streambed called a wadi. Now, he saw that most of the firing was coming from the right bank of the wadi. He also saw that some of his own troops were in trouble because their grenade launcher had jammed. Risso grabbed another rifle, an M4, and fired a heavy blast of constant gunfire with the two rifles. Ducking his streams of

The M16: The Standard Since 1962

bullets, the opposing side was unable to shoot back. By the time the convoy commander was able to get the vehicles moving again, Risso had fired more than 150 rounds of ammunition.

Using American weapons, Major Risso had helped the Americans and British fight their way out of the ambush. The good design of the M16 he had picked up made it a simple, reliable weapon to use. It helped make his actions successful. For those brave actions, Major Colin Risso was awarded the British Military Cross.

Making the M16 Better

In 1962, the US Army adopted the first version of the M16 (called the M16A1), and it became the standard weapon for soldiers heading to Vietnam beginning in 1965. Soldiers using today's updated M16 have a better rifle because of the lessons learned the hard way with the M16A1.

In Vietnam, rain, mud, sweat, and grit got into the M16A1 rifles and gummed up their working parts. The rifles had to be taken apart and cleaned with a special kit that every soldier carried. Also, the breech into which the cartridges were fed from the magazine became rusty. Empty cartridge cases jammed in the breech and had to be pried out with a knife. Many soldiers were killed or wounded because their rifles jammed during a fight and they could not defend themselves.

American rifle designers worked on the problems as fast as they were reported. The rusted breeches were plated with chrome to stop rust. New stronger, long-lasting magazines to hold ammunition were assembled. A muzzle "brake" was added to the front of the barrel. This brake kept the muzzle from rising every time the rifle fired by blowing gas from each shot upward. By keeping the rifle steady, the brake allowed a soldier to keep the sights on the target.

Full automatic fire was replaced by three-shot bursts of fire with each trigger pull. This saved ammunition and still allowed firepower when needed in close quarters or facing crowds of attacking enemy soldiers.

FACT

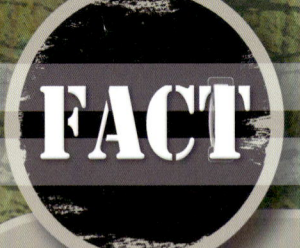

The General's Dessert

Chunks of red pulp flew into the air as the bullet struck. Another shot banged from the rifle, and a second splash of red stained the grass. The general lowered his smoking weapon and squinted at the third target. "We'll eat that last watermelon for dessert," he said. In July 1960, Robert MacDonald of Colt Industries, who wanted to manufacture the new rifle invented by Eugene Stoner, invited Air Force general Curtis LeMay to a birthday party. LeMay was asked to try the rifle. Three watermelons were set up outside at different ranges as targets. LeMay fired twice and exploded two of the melons, saving the third for dessert.

Back in Washington, General LeMay told Secretary of Defense Robert S. McNamara about the new rifle. LeMay ordered 8,500 of the rifles for air force police units. Soon, after more design changes, the new weapon became the famous M16.

General LeMay

The M16: The Standard Since 1962

Military personnel inspect an M16.

It was very hard to see the opposing forces in the dim jungle light or near dawn and twilight. A special "light-gathering" sight was designed for the M16 that made the scene seem brighter under dim conditions so soldiers could more easily see their targets.

For additional firepower an M203 grenade launcher could be attached beneath the barrel of the M16A1. This launcher acted like a small cannon that fires a 40mm explosive, tear gas, or smoke grenade. The 15-inch tube could be attached in the field or could remain on the M16 rifle, adding only 3 pounds (1.36 kg) to the rifle's weight. The M203 grenade launcher gave soldiers a powerful weapon against lightly armored trucks, machine guns, heavy doors, or when firing into buildings to stop opposing fire.

As the improvements arrived on the battlefield, soldiers became more confident with their rifles. The changes resulted in a second version of the M16 called the M16A2, introduced in the early 1980s. The M16A2 became the standard rifle of the US Army and Marine Corps until the M4 rifle replaced it in 2003. The basic design of the M16 has gone on to become the longest serving rifle in US military history.

FACT

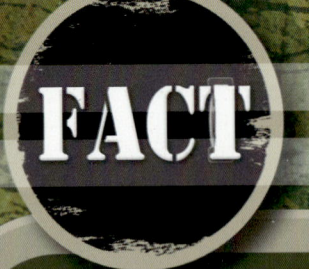

Who Produced the M16?

When the M16 was first issued to American soldiers, they were used to a heavier rifle with a wooden stock and steel moving parts. Soldiers thought the lightweight aluminum M16 with its plastic stock seemed more like a toy. In the 1960s, the toy company Mattell actually did produce the "Marauder," a toy M16 that looked like the real thing. This helped fuel a myth that the real M16 was also made by the toy company, but Colt Manufacturing was the maker of the real M16.

M16 rifle

CHAPTER 4

The M4 and Combat Rifles of the Future

Air Force staff sergeant Kevin Donell Vance was near his Chinook helicopter's back door when opposing ground fire suddenly slammed into his chopper, sending it into a turning, twisting spiral. The Chinook, along with its twenty-one crew members, crashed to the ground.

Sergeant Vance's helicopter was on a rescue mission in Afghanistan on March 4, 2002, to bring back an American soldier who had fallen from another helicopter during an earlier mission. Many of the crew members on the Chinook, including the pilot, were injured, and Vance was the only uninjured man on board with combat training. He quickly directed the crew members who could still shoot to defend the chopper, while he tried to contact his base to get help. Afghan soldiers fired from a nearby building. Their bullets thudded against the downed helicopter's metal skin and dug furrows in the

MILITARY RIFLES: Combat Ready

dusty soil around it. The chopper's windows shattered. The smell of fuel and hot oil was heavy in the air.

"I was shooting an M4. At first, I had to keep firing at the enemy, to hold them back and then to find help for CAS [close air support] on the radio," Vance wrote later.

While Vance's wounded crewmen tried to communicate with their base, he was under constant enemy automatic weapon fire. "First, we shot M203 rounds at a bunker," Vance wrote. "An M203 is a grenade launcher that fits on a M4/16. As the squad leader and team leader shot M203s, I stood up and provided covering fire. When he would stand up to fire a grenade at the bunker, I would stand up and shoot at the bunker to cover him. I did the same when the crew members would run for more ammo [ammunition]."

A shorter version of the M16, the M4 rifle can adapt to many combat situations.

FACT

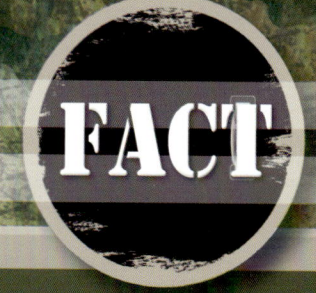

Insurgent Weapons

American soldiers often have to fight against terrorists and insurgents, or fighters who rebel against authority. These fighters get their weapons from many sources around the world. In the Middle East, many insurgents use the AK-47 Kalishnikov rifle, including the Somali pirates who captured the captain of the merchant ship MV *Maersk Alabama* in 2009, Captain Richard Phillips. It is an assault rifle that was created in Russia following World War II. The AK-47 is one of the best military rifles ever designed. It is durable, easy to shoot, and inexpensive to build.

Insurgents also often use rocket-propelled grenade (RPG) launchers. The grenade is a missile with fins to guide it. The special explosive inside the grenade can destroy lightly armored vehicles, sandbag protection, and most building construction.

Insurgents and terrorists also make their own weapons. Improvised explosive devices (IEDs), for example, are buried near roads. They are set off with remote-control radio signals or cell phones when a vehicle passes by.

Other homemade bombs are packed with scraps of metal, nails, and tiny steel balls. When they explode, the small, sharp objects are forcefully sent in every direction. These homemade bombs are extremely dangerous.

Vance fought for thirteen hours until air strikes by F-15 fighter planes and reinforcements arrived. The rescue mission had turned into a full-scale battle. Covering gunfire finally allowed Chinook helicopters to land and rescue the fifteen survivors.

"I went through so many different emotions: excited, mad, frustrated, sad, any other emotion you could possibly feel," Vance wrote after the fight.

The M4: Shorter Version of the M16

When the marines wanted a version of the M16 that could be used as a close quarters battle (CQB) weapon, the M4 rifle was developed. Originally requested by the US Marine Corps in 1983 as part of a modular weapons system (MWS) program, the M16 design was shortened by trimming back the barrel and making the stock collapsible. The new rifle was only 26 inches (66 centimeters) long compared to the almost 40-inch-long (101.6 cm) M16.

The M4 was given to tank crews who needed shorter weapons to carry in their tanks' cramped spaces. The latest version of the M4, the M4A1, is now being given to troops fighting the war in Iraq because much of the fighting takes place in cities and villages instead of wide-open spaces. Patrols moving through narrow streets and houses carry the M4A1 rifle to stop ambushes and clear out opposing snipers.

The Future of Military Rifles

Since the American Revolutionary War, the US military has tried to build better and better weapons using the latest technology available. Engineers and scientists at the US Army's Picatinny Arsenal weapons research and development center in New Jersey are constantly working to do this. These new and better weapons will improve the effectiveness and combat survival of all military personnel.

According to Picatinny designers, the newest military rifles have "airburst" grenade launch capability and advanced electronic

FACT

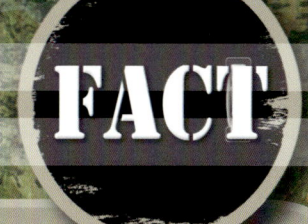

Airburst Rifles

Field tested with soldiers in Afghanistan in 2010 and scheduled to be officially introduced in late 2015, the XM25 Counter Defilade Target Engagement (CDTE) System is an "airburst" grenade launcher. The weapon fires 25mm grenades that explode in mid-air at or near the target. Using "smart technology," a laser rangefinder inside the weapon determines how far away the target is and tracks the distance the grenade travels. The grenade is detonated at the perfect distance to produce an airburst effect, making it more efficient to hit targets that are hidden or under the ground.

XM25 SPECIFICATIONS
WEIGHT: 14 pounds (6.4 kg)
OPERATION: Gas-operated, semiautomatic
CALIBER: Low-velocity 25mm

An XM25 airburst rifle cobines the capabilities of a rifle and a grenade launcher.

MILITARY RIFLES: Combat Ready

sighting, which allow soldiers to shoot further. The XM25 Counter Defilade Target Engagement (CDTE) System, which uses "smart technology," combines the capabilities of a rifle and a grenade launcher.

The XM25 and other new weapons will lighten the soldier's load, reducing exhaustion over long marches. This will allow soldiers to complete their missions more easily and successfully. As they have for centuries, US soldiers in the future will be able to defend themselves and the freedom of others with the best weapons in the world.

The XM25 rifle was designed with smart technology.

FACT

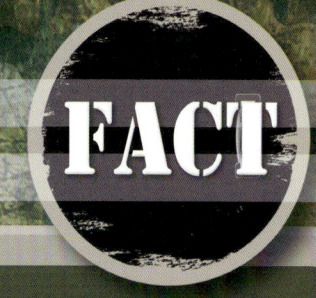

The M4A1 Rifle

The new M4A1 rifles are very adaptable to many combat situations. The carry handle rear sight that is a feature on all M16s and M4s can be removed. It improves the sight pictures and enhances the accuracy of the shot. A flat cover called a Picatinny rail can then be installed. The army calls this the Rail Interface System (RIS), which allows a variety of attachments, such as sights, lasers, flashlights, and other devices to be added to the rifle.

    Some sights available for the M4A1 use a laser pointer. A laser pointer is a tiny projector that shows a red mark on the target at the point where the bullet will strike. Other sighting devices allow a soldier to see targets at night. The M4A1 is becoming the standard-issue military rifle for American soldiers.

CHAPTER 5

Saved by a Sniper

It was now day five into Captain Richard Phillips's ordeal. Captured by Somali pirates in the Gulf of Aden on April 8, 2009, Captain Richard Phillips and his crew of the merchant ship MV *Maersk Alabama* were being held for ransom. A small group of crew members had managed to overpower one of the pirates and lock themselves in the ship's engine room. They attempted to exchange this pirate for their ship's captain, Captain Phillips. Refusing, the pirates escaped the scene in a small lifeboat with Captain Phillips as their hostage. A tense standoff ensued between the heavily armed pirates and two US Navy ships, the destroyer USS *Bainbridge* and the frigate USS *Halyburton*, that were dispatched to the scene.

Now, five days later, on April 12, both Captain Phillips and his captors were weary. As he described in his book, *A Captain's Story*, Captain Phillips said, "When I woke up Sunday morning, the boat was dark, gloomy. It matched my mood." The pirates were also moody and had started fighting among themselves that day; clearly, their resolve to exact an American ransom was fraying. And Captain Phillips knew it. So, he started to act more defiant around them. "I kicked the ropes free from my feet and stood up. The pirates' heads popped up from fore and aft. I walked forward." He told them he wasn't going to play their game anymore and he was leaving. He knew they wouldn't shoot him, as they would lose all negotiating power with the Americans. But they could scare him.

Then, BOOOM! A shot rang out, coming from the front of the small boat. One of the pirates had shot his AK-47 semiautomatic rifle in the air in anger. The situation was clearly deteriorating. Meanwhile, Navy SEAL snipers were aboard the *Bainbridge* trying to get a clear aim at the three pirates, but it was difficult because the space on the lifeboat was small and they didn't want to hit Captain Phillips. They had been waiting and waiting, but now the crisis took on a more urgent tone.

"I went to lie down on the makeshift bed. As I turned, I saw [two of the pirates] walk up toward the forward hatch. . . . They were raising themselves up as I slid down to the floor. I was exhausted. I just wanted to rest. All of a sudden, shots rang out. Bangbangbang-bangbangbang." And then silence.

Captain Phillips wasn't sure if the pirates had shot at each other. Then, he heard an American voice, asking him if he was okay. Captain Phillips looked around him and saw three dead pirates and a Navy SEAL standing over him. The ordeal was over.

The sharpshooters who took out the pirates were highly trained. The weapon they most likely used to kill the pirates, the semiautomatic special application sniper rifle—the Stoner Rifle-25 (SR-25)—is one of the most technologically advanced of today's modern rifles.

The History of Snipers in the Military

American snipers were first used effectively during the Revolutionary War. They used the first rifles that could hit a target at a range of about 300 yards (275 m) using a long rifled barrel. But the military thought these sharpshooting soldiers were "murderers"

MILITARY RIFLES: Combat Ready

US Army snipers keep watch while locals hold a town meeting in Dey Yak, Afghanistan.

and "assassins" who hunted their targets from trees and from behind fences. Armies at that time and also during the Civil War usually stood and faced each other, firing their rifles as a group on command.

Snipers were very effective, and all armies used them. Even so, at the end of every war all sniper training stopped because commanders considered the extra training unnecessary and too expensive.

Today, both the US Army and Marine Corps have permanent sniper training schools and use snipers in warfare. American snipers are trained to defeat opposing snipers. They hit individual targets at great distances, forcing the other side to stay undercover.

Saved by a Sniper

Snipers can also knock out opposing vehicles from as far away as 1,500 meters (1,640 yards) with the largest rifle used in today's combat. Their shooting skills have saved many American and civilian lives.

The Army's Sniper Rifle

In 1986, the US Army held trials to find out what manufacturer made the best rifle for use as a sniper weapon. The award went to the Remington Arms Company for a version of its popular hunting rifle. With many changes, it became the M24 sniper rifle.

A single shot "bolt action" was designed for the rifle. This action loads a new, full cartridge from the magazine into the breech after

A US Marine Corps corporal looks through the scope of a 12.7mm Barrett Light Fifty Model 82A1 sniping rifle.

FACT

Bigger Rifle, Longer Range

In the 1980s, Ronald Barrett designed a ten-shot semiautomatic weapon that used a large 13mm cartridge. Today, these Barrett M82A1 and M99 Heavy Sniper weapons are used in Iraq and Afghanistan as long-range rifles that can knock out lightly armored equipment, cars, or trucks from 5,000 to 10,000 feet (1,500 to 3,000 m).

The M82A1 is large and heavy. It weighs 33.8 pounds (15.3 kg) and is 57 inches (145 cm)—almost 5 feet (1.5 m)—long. Two legs extend beneath the rifle's muzzle to help support its weight. A target a mile away is no longer out of range.

On the end of this M82A1 is an attachment that decreases the rifle's recoil and also hides the flash produced by the rifle as it fires. This helps the sniper to stay hidden.

M82A1

each shot. The trigger, heavy barrel, and very powerful telescopic sight of the M24 are designed based on the rifles used in the shooting contests of the Olympic Games. With the telescopic sight, a distant target can be seen clearly. It also allows a marksman to make very fine adjustments so the shot will be as accurate as possible.

For combat use in jungle mud, desert sand, and rocky areas, every part is made stronger. The weather-proof shoulder stock is custom fitted to each sniper so the rifle can be held rock steady on a target. The M24 rifle weighs 12 pounds (5.4 kg). Snipers must be in top physical shape to carry both their rifle and their full field equipment every day.

The Marine Corps' Sniper Rifle

In 1966, the marines were already using the Remington Olympic-quality target rifle as their model M40 sniper weapon. In the 1970s, the marines added a stronger plastic stock and a better telescopic sight. The M40 was now the M40A1, but by the 1990s, the marines wanted to design a new rifle from scratch.

The result was the M40A3 sniper rifle. This model uses the same bolt action as the army M24 rifle. The marines added a shoulder stock that can be adjusted in the field.

FACT

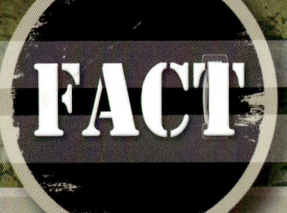

The Ultimate Rifle Test

Every year at Camp Perry, Ohio, rifle competitions are held. These competitions test the finest US military and civilian marksmen and markswomen. The National Trophy Team Match is one event in the competition. It is nicknamed the "Rattle Battle" because of the large amount of ammunition fired in a short period of time.

In the Rattle Battle, teams must shoot at eight targets while firing from a prone, or lying down, position at 600 yards (549 m) and 500 yards (457 m). (The Rattle Battle is a civilian-sponsored event, so US measurements are used instead of metric measurements.) When the teams move to the 300-yard (274 m) line, they must shoot from a sitting position. If they have any ammunition left, they fire the remaining rounds in a standing position at 200 yards (183 m). At each stage, they have fifty seconds to fire as many accurate shots as they can.

Members of a team fire from a prone position during a sniper competition.

CHAPTER 6

Developing Shooting Skills

Rifle training has changed as the role of ground troops has changed, but the basic skills are the same. All military services offer marksmanship training for new service members. The rifle is only as good as the soldier who uses it, so today's average combat soldier must be effective at firing at many different types of targets and ranges.

When they enter the military, even the most experienced civilian hunters and target shooters have to learn the mechanics of combat shooting if they are going to survive or be able to support their fellow soldiers. The US Army and Marine Corps stress effective and safe rifle handling for soldiers because that is their primary job.

Skills learned on a rifle range become life-saving reflexes in combat. Mastering the combat rifle also builds self-confidence in civilian life.

Soldiers learn to quickly set their rifle sights on targets at various distances: as close as 25 meters (82 feet) and as far away as

MILITARY RIFLES: Combat Ready

300 meters (984 feet). They also learn how to handle their weapons safely when not fighting. Today's rifle training teaches soldiers how to recognize targets on city streets and inside buildings. Under the stress of combat, it is often difficult to tell innocent civilians from dangerous opponents.

Marksmanship Training

Army and marine training teaches recruits the basics of marksmanship with their service rifle. Both branches use similar training techniques. This training takes place over two weeks, the first of which is called Snap-In Week. During this week, recruits practice shooting from four positions (standing, kneeling, sitting, and prone, or lying down). A primary marksmanship instructor shows recruits how to fire, how to adjust their sights, how to take into account the effects of the weather, and other shooting skills. Recruits also have the chance to fire on the Indoor Simulated Marksmanship Training (ISMT) machine.

Marksmanship training took place in Kuwait before the personnel were deployed to Afghanistan.

FACT

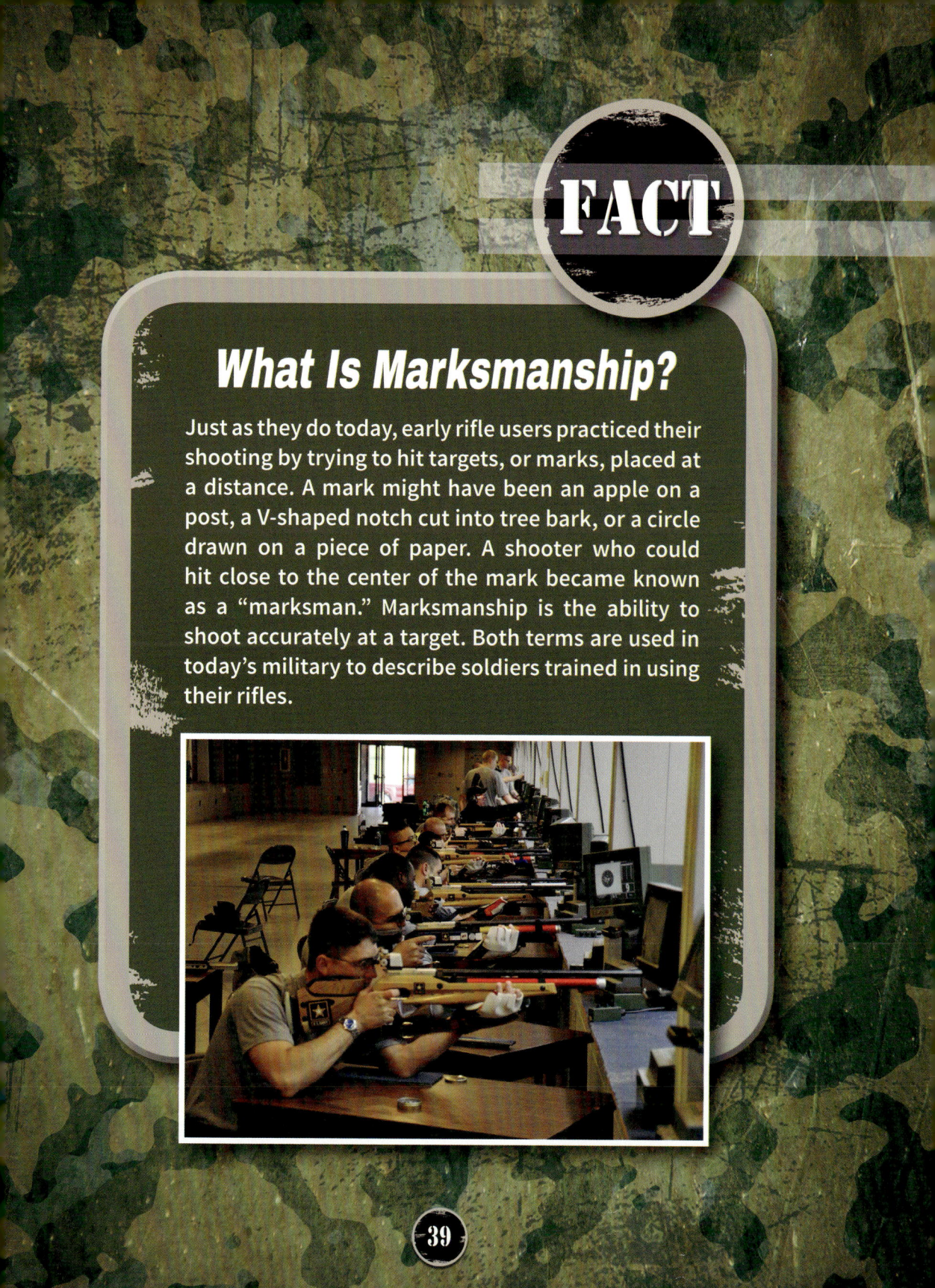

What Is Marksmanship?

Just as they do today, early rifle users practiced their shooting by trying to hit targets, or marks, placed at a distance. A mark might have been an apple on a post, a V-shaped notch cut into tree bark, or a circle drawn on a piece of paper. A shooter who could hit close to the center of the mark became known as a "marksman." Marksmanship is the ability to shoot accurately at a target. Both terms are used in today's military to describe soldiers trained in using their rifles.

MILITARY RIFLES: Combat Ready

At an ISMT range, trainees fire laser-fitted weapons at simulated targets that are projected onto large screens. There are also "shoot/no-shoot" exercises, where a simulated enemy is shown standing next to a simulated innocent civilian. It helps soldiers know how to recognize and react to such situations.

During the second week of marksmanship training, recruits actually fire rifles on a course—at ranges of 75, 175, and 300 meters (246, 574, and 984 ft). Recruits prepare for a test, or rifle qualification, on Friday of that week.

When this basic rifle training is complete, Field Firing Range (FFR) training begins. FFR is devoted to firing weapons in more realistic conditions. During earlier marksmanship training, recruits learn how to fire at a single target from one location. During FFR, recruits learn how to fire at moving and multiple targets, while under low-light conditions and wearing their field protective (gas) mask. This mask is designed to protect the soldier in the field from breathing harmful gases used as weapons. The mask covers the soldier's face. The soldier sees out through two clear plastic lenses and breathes through an air filter. It is difficult to see to the left or the right. It can be hot and sweaty inside the mask. The recruit must learn to fire without being able to wipe his or her eyes. Recruits are trained to shoot while peering through this dusty plastic with poor vision to the sides—a difficult task.

To graduate from marksmanship training, a recruit must score at a certain level in order to earn one of three designations: marksman, sharpshooter, or expert rifleman. The highest award, an expert rifleman designation, can be the first step to becoming a sniper. The higher the designation a soldier earns, the better the opportunity for advancement in rank. Soldiers can request to take the test again to try to improve their score if necessary.

A soldier in rifle training develops skills such as self-discipline, physical control of muscle groups, eye-hand coordination, and responsibility for handling a deadly weapon in a safe manner at all times. Learning the rules of safe rifle handling and taking

FACT

Rifle Qualification

Every soldier must qualify as an infantry rifleman on the training rifle range with an M16 or M4. To qualify means that a soldier must fire a certain number of shots at targets set up at different ranges. The rifle must be fired from different positions, too: prone, kneeling, sitting, and standing.

Each target is marked so the soldier receives a certain number of points, depending on where the target is hit. A center hit gets five points. A hit near the edge of the target gets only one point. The soldier must get a minimum number of points to qualify at each range. The higher the number of points, the higher the qualification the soldier receives, from marksman to sharpshooter to the highest, expert.

Lining Up the Sights

Every military rifle has a front and a rear sight. During training, a recruit is taught how to combine, or align, these two sights and then place this "sight picture" on the target. When the front sight is positioned in the hole of the rear sight, this "alignment" is placed over the target to make the sight picture.

Then the trigger is squeezed until the rifle fires. Soldiers learn that it is important to slowly squeeze the trigger, not jerk or yank it. Jerking or yanking the trigger moves the sight alignment off the target, spoiling the sight picture at the instant of firing. Jerking the trigger also moves the barrel away from the target, and the bullet will miss.

Looking down the sight of an M16A2 rifle

Developing Shooting Skills

A US Army soldier makes an adjustment to his M-4 rifle during combat training.

responsibility for the safety of those nearby is an important life skill. Soldiers learn that carrying a rifle is a badge of honor with a long tradition of courage and pride. These qualities translate into any civilian career path once a soldier's military career has ended.

Driving a car, using power tools, or mastering a difficult sports technique all require practice and learning each step to reach a goal. Rifle training is even more demanding. Once a bullet leaves the barrel it can travel over a mile and injure someone the shooter cannot even see. Rifle marksmen always know where their weapon is pointed. They always make sure that their weapon is safe when not actually pointed at a target. They know they hold the lives of other people in their hands.

For US soldiers, navy sailors, or marines, successful training is part of their duty to themselves, their unit, and their country.

> Mastering a powerful weapon such as a rifle is a great responsibility and a great honor.

TIMELINE

9th century—Chinese invent gunpowder and the predecessor to the modern firearm, the "fire lance."

1775–1783—American colonial soldiers first use hunting weapons with "rifling."

1936—The first semiautomatic rifle is invented by John Garand.

1962—The US Army first adopts the M16, which becomes the standard weapon for the US Army and Marine Corps in Vietnam.

2002—The M4 rifle is introduced.

2015—The XM25 airburst grenade launcher is scheduled to be introduced.

GLOSSARY

action—The collection of mechanical parts that make a rifle shoot.

airburst grenade launcher—A weapon that uses smart technology to direct and fire 25mm grenades that explode in mid-air at or near a target.

barrel—The tube down which a bullet travels out of a rifle.

bolt—A sliding block that seals the rear of a rifle when the rifle fires. The bolt slides to the rear, removing the empty cartridge case, and is then slid forward to feed a fresh cartridge from the rifle's magazine into the breech.

breech—The rear of a rifle's barrel, where ammunition is loaded to be fired.

carry handle rear sight—A removable rifle sight that improves the sight pictures and enhances the accuracy of the shot.

cartridge—A small case that contains a rifle's ammunition and propellant. Also called a round.

civilian—A person who is not a professional soldier.

fire lance—The predecessor to all modern firearms. A weapon that combined a spear with a mounted bamboo tube containing gunpowder and a small projectile or a poison dart.

grenade—A small bomb that can be thrown by hand or fired from a launcher.

magazine—A box loaded with ammunition that fits into a rifle.

marksmanship—The ability to hit a target with a shot from a certain distance.

muzzle—The front end of a rifle barrel.

night vision—A system of battery-powered goggles, binoculars, or rifle sights that increase a soldier's ability to see at night by electronically magnifying the available light.

range—The distance from one point to another.

sight—A hole on a rifle that a shooter looks through to aim the rifle at a target.

stock—The part of a rifle that is held against a shooter's shoulder and cheek.

trigger—The part of a rifle that is squeezed to start the action of the rifle's firing.

FURTHER READING

BOOKS

Kyle, Chris, Jim DeFelice, and Scott McEwan. *American Sniper.* New York: William Morrow Publishers, 2012.

Owen, Mark, and Kevin Maurer. *No Easy Day: The Autobiography of a Navy SEAL.* New York: Penguin Group, 2012.

Phillips, Richard, and Stephan Talty. *A Captain's Duty: Somali Pirates, Navy SEALs, and Dangerous Days at Sea.* New York: Hyperion Books, 2010.

WEB SITES

marines.com
  Marine Corps recruiting Web site.

navyseals.com/weapons-demo
  Navy SEAL recruiting Web site with descriptions of firearms they use.

pica.army.mil/PicatinnyPublic/products_services/index.asp
  The US Army's Picatinny Arsenal describes the various rifles it develops.

M16 Rifle

INDEX

A
action, 11
airburst grenade launcher, 26, 27
AK-47, 25, 31
ammunition, 10, 14, 19, 24, 36
Army, US, 6, 14, 15, 17, 19, 21, 26, 32, 33, 35, 37, 38
automatic fire, 14, 19

B
barrels, 11, 12, 14, 21, 26, 35
bin Laden, Osama, 5–6
breech, 11, 14, 19, 35

C
calibers, 10
cartridges, 14, 19, 34, 35
Civil War, 14, 17, 32
Colt, 20, 22

F
Field Firing Range (FFR) Training, 40
field protective (gas) masks, 40
fire lance, 12

G
Garand, John, 14
gunpowder, 12, 14
guns, 9

I
Indoor Simulated Marksmanship Training (ISMT) machines, 38, 40
insurgents, 25

K
Korean War, 14

L
LeMay, Curtis, 20

M
M1 rifles, 14, 15
M4 rifles, 6–8, 9, 18, 21, 24, 26, 29, 41
M16 rifles, 8, 15, 18, 19–21, 22, 24, 26, 29, 41
M24 sniper rifles, 33, 35
M40 rifles, 35
M82 rifles, 34
M99 rifles, 34
M203 grenade launchers, 21, 24
magazines, 11, 14, 19, 35
Marine Corps, US, 6, 17, 21, 26, 32, 35, 37, 38
marksmanship, 35, 36, 37, 38, 39, 40, 41
muzzles, 10, 11, 14, 19

P
Phillips, Richard, 25, 30–31

Picatinny rail, 29

Q
qualifications, 41

R
Remington, 33, 35
Revolutionary War, 8, 14, 26, 31–32
rounds, 14, 19, 24, 36

S
SEALs, 5–6, 17, 31
semiautomatic weapons, 14, 31, 34
sights, 11, 21, 29, 35, 42
snipers, 14, 16, 17, 31–35, 40
stocks, 11, 15, 22, 26, 35
Stoner, Eugene, 14–15, 20

T
training, 37–43
triggers, 11, 15, 35, 42

V
Vietnam War, 14, 17, 19

W
World War II, 14, 15

X
XM25, 27, 28